The Rape Poems

The Rape Poems

Frances Driscoll

Frances Driscoll

Pleasure Boat Studio

Grateful acknowledgement is made to the editors of the following periodicals where some of the poems originally appeared: *Go, International Quarterly, The Massachusetts Review, Pudding, Sojourner, 13th Moon, Volt* and *Willow Springs.*

"Island Of The Raped Women," nominated by *Volt,* appeared in THE PUSHCART PRIZE, XIX: BEST OF THE SMALL PRESSES.

Mudlark published a chapbook of some of the poems.

Design and Composition by Fred Elliott
Cover photograph by Jeanie Rini Slaughter

Published by Pleasure Boat Studio
802 East Sixth
Port Angeles, WA 98362

Tel-Fax: (360) 452-8686
E-mail: pbstudio@pbstudio.com
URL: http://www.pbstudio.com

ISBN 0-9651413-1-4
LCCN 96-72150

Printed in the United States of America by Thomson-Shore

First Edition

for

Constance

Martha, Sara, Maribeth
Elizabeth and Maya

for

Justine

Justine
Rachel and Heather Dawn

Contents

No One Writes Me

from Thérèse Plantier

No one writes me. I am waiting. No one writes me. I am waiting for a horse blue as a star and as able to bleed. I am waiting to follow air tracing a woman's smile.

What if I walk on my hands and when hands wear away on wrists elbows belly eyes what is self worn to what is left of a woman kept on a barroom table used in a foreign language there.

Reading Material

In the heart of the lightning belt, enamored
of humidity—the wet ruin it makes of everything—
my sister reads to the head-injured who can only
blink or nod. Her goal is consistent response.
When I ask what she reads, she will not tell.
My sister, being my sister, just laughs. Laughs until
I laugh too. In the early days, daily laughter
a memory I did not remember, the familiar form
of recipes calmed my breathing. Bee balm salad.
What to do with wild plums in season. News was then
and remains a risk. Even when old: The November 1964
Farmington Valley Herald weekly my mother sends
because it contains notice my sister's second grade
class is going on a field trip. (My mother
knows I will save anything anybody else has saved
that many years.) But buried in the police
report. Buried after the reports of drivers failing
to maintain reasonable distance apart, buried
after the reports of drivers operating without mudflaps,
I find a young girl kept in a tobacco shed the six days
she was missing from her home. Turning from the page,
I can not turn from her, from the light streaking in
between those dark weathered boards, fracturing,
splintering upon reaching the dried blood, earth
marking the slender golden length of her. I find

in her eyes what I found in the eyes of my own mirror.
Until I just plain stopped looking. I could not
stand what was there, not there. What I still have
no language to describe. Reaching for contemporary
distraction, I read in Texas of interest in investing
in functional clay. I don't know what functional
clay means, but love the sound of it in my mouth. But
above the fold on Page 1, begins a story we know: Men
with eyes of sharks, wiped fingerprints, slipped
away, the Associated Press reports, leaving hostages
to stumble newly blind, emerging trembling into
desert morning darkness from a prison of fear
they will carry now with them. I remember this. This
forgetting of ways to move. What was left
of that night, I could only crawl. We could talk here
of loss. We might incorporate a discussion
of deconstructivist architecture. The irreconcilable.
The deranged. The deformed. The tilted. The warped.
The unsettling. Sabotaged notions of stability.
Contorted interiors reflecting the disquiet of our
world. Designed to cause pain. Keeping me pinned
to my own floor required somehow only three limbs.
One hand was free for what he wanted. Please, I said.
Please. I could not say that word again for a long
time without immediate need of those good pills. But
I can say that word now and still get some sleep

the same night. Some small things are returned to us
given enough time and careful care. For example, when
Barbara Louise gave me camomile soap, I remained
longer then under water. But, 1,572 days later, when
a man with truly wonderful hair who reads
about parrots in the wild and other interesting things
says—and from an appropriate distance—could I have
a birthday hug. I say, No. Move sideways. Away.
Barbara also gave me clear pink rose-perfumed soap.
The rose you know is in the peach family. I have
a wonderful recipe for peach ice cream.

Ray's Sentence

I do this all the time, he said.
I ruin everything. I ruin everything.

Parochial Air

Prescription drugs do well here. Normal
balance seems easily disturbed.
Karen's neck is bothering her again and
I am suffering in this city which,
for all its humidity, has never had
a major Star Trek convention with
inflammation the physician's assistant
found by hand. The things we pay to have
done to us while perfectly good dresses
hang on sale racks. I don't need
inflammation explained. What is there
to do with evidence but burn it. We all
know the temperature of sin. And so
these blue pills are for vaginitis and
oval with patience these help me sleep
when I let them. Also they keep the
dreams from me leaving me with only
this steaming local air to contend with
in the dark. Things form in this climate,
my therapist explains, unknown further
north. Calm talk of fungus follows. He
means to suggest I suppose this condition
I am carrying on so about in extreme
language may have nothing to do with the
man who first dropped to his knees.
Sniffed at me like an animal or a man
gone mad. I just want to smell it, he said,
but he lied.

Dreams Of Girls

The cat's never had much in the way of a sweet tooth,
my son remarks, slowing his way to bed to feed
the dog peanut butter cookies. Leaving me
making my way through a bag of probably sprayed plums
most likely picked by girlchild illiterate labor, reluctant
again or as usual to turn from the light, give myself
over to this bed sheeted in blue imitation impressionism.
I don't know why I never thought to try food.
Offer him something sweet. That sounds so unlike me.
Not at all the way I was brought up. I remember
early and simple beds. Beds my grandmother made
up the curved stairs in her brown shingled house. Soft.
High. White. Rosary-laced posts. How after good-night
tea and a little sweet something—fruit sliced into
cream with ladyfingers or, sometimes, if the season
and the afternoon had been right, blueberry cake—
we slept there with her. So many girls. Slipping
into wishes inside her rose-printed long flannel gowns.
All bundled together. Waiting for stories to flavor
our dreams. The Persian lamb: Their baby sister stricken
with great fever, our grandmother Mamie and her sister
Margaret bargained with Our Blessed Mother for Sally's
life—weeks of their mill pay pledged to the mission
of keeping Sally all dolled up in finery. And that
is how Sally acquired that grand fur wrap. Romance
in a woolen mill town: How the paymaster courted

her nightly over chess with her father while she sewed
alone in her room upstairs. And that is how middling
in her thirties our grandmother consented to leave
one house for one of her own. I never saw John naked,
she said, discussing the then-current sexual revolution,
and I never wanted to. I never wanted to. When he comes
back, as he does so often, I try to see him still
in the brown polyester slacks. But my luck's gone
bad. My wishes all run out. Used up on the one: Please,
just don't let him kill me. Please, just don't let him.
Please. Just. Don't. Just a few hours of just one night.
A Wednesday in a February that would have been ordinary.
Had it not been my grandmother's birthday. Had it not been
for a man concerned with my comfort. Is my zipper
bothering you, he said, well into the second hour on the
floor. I don't want to hurt you. By then, nothing hurt
and nothing resembling sound would come out of me.
I tried mouthing the word, No, tried moving my head
the way we do in this country and perhaps in other
countries when what we mean is: No. But he gave
what he wanted to give. Took away the dark
metal teeth grinding against me. Engraved the memory
of those legs that went on forever. Those legs
that keep coming and coming back to me. Hard
as New Hampshire granite. Material meant to last.
I lap plum juice from my wrist, my arm. The sky

considering blue again, I dare risk my face sinking
into one of my grandmother's feather down pillows
flattened with the years, with the dreams of girls.
Sniffing for sleep all those first and darkest
months, more than fully clothed and wrapped
in my son's faded flannel robe—an ensemble hard
to sustain this far south—I could close
my eyes only to the face of my therapist.
Drift with golden skin a cameraman would die for,
backlighting washing through masses of golden wavy hair.
I lost that good keeper of the vigil some time ago now
to a pale man with straight brown hair. No
resemblance to the Christ nor any archangel. Not even
a minor saint. Now, I envision doughnuts
from the Dip 'N' Sip down the street. Powdered
sugar. Coconut. Angel cream. I dream of a bed. White.
With girls.

Incomplete Examination

Until I say—no, no more—the physician specifically
trained for such occasions, examines me naked late
the next afternoon, inch by careful inch, slowly
touching me slowly everywhere slowly. You are
ovulating, he says. He has pills for that, among
other things. He remarks upon raw skin, bruises. Keeps
finding bruise after bruise. I can not connect bruises
with what happened and I can not talk any more. Old,
I say, fall down. I can not talk any more. I have
already talked with the center director, the
policewoman, the center director, the psychologist,
the center director. I can not talk any more.
Could I describe the rape for him, he says. Minor, I say.
Ordinary.

Difficult Word

Sodomy, Kate says, sodomy. That's such a difficult word.
But it is such an easier word to say than to say
what he said, what he said could happen, what did happen.
And Kate, this is so difficult to say it takes me
years to begin to try to say this part of the story.
How after inhuman time, the erection begins to leave him. How
I pretend not to notice. Until now, I have been trying only
not to move. If I want to avoid anal sex,
I have been instructed not to move. This is when he is
slamming himself into me. I am even more afraid now. I am
so afraid now, Kate. I am so afraid. I believe if he believes
I don't know maybe he will not kill me. Now he is using his hands
to shove himself into me. This part seems to last
a long time. And now he is off me. He is
stretched out, propped on one elbow. He looks perfectly
comfortable, Kate. He looks like everything is normal here, Kate.
Kate, he is going to kill me, Kate. He gestures down,
You're going to have to, he says. You're going
to have to. He sounds so sad saying this. Like
if it were up to him, he wouldn't be saying this. He's crazy,
Kate. He's really really crazy. And this will not
work. He has not been a boy for a long time and he has had me
down on the floor for a long time. This will not work.
And when this does not work, he will kill me. I know this.
I run. I run very very fast, Kate. But really Kate, I am not
running. And really I am not even crawling. Really I am trying

to slither myself along the way you sometimes in TV movies
see soldiers under fire move. And really Kate,
it is only inches that I do move. Like used dishwater,
there is nothing left of me now. I am going to die, Katie.
And he leans only slightly, uses only one arm to draw me to him.
You're going to have to, he says, and his palm pushes my head
down.

Donor Mentality

The dog has a skin condition and addicted
as I am to my therapist with twice a week
being almost not enough to get by I can not
decide whether to warn him crossing
his legs the way he does leads straight
to varicose veins of the worst sort.
Defeating to my mind benefits of that
stressless chair. Things come apart
in this climate, the dishwasher repairman
explains. Parts can be ordered. Exactly
my first thought stumbling in the dark
I still have such trouble giving myself to
with the operator repeating Collect call
from Majorca. Collect call from Majorca.
I assumed urgent transatlantic need
for perhaps my bone marrow but it was only
Jim wanting to know how I am and better
was not the right answer. Better did not
satisfy Jim who turned out to be a wrong
number anyway but perhaps an honest one
although the phone bill has yet to arrive.

But Remember.

I turn 39. I wasn't worried until my son said,
Don't worry. I'm just tickling her behind her right
knee. I don't think just because somebody sticks
a sword in somebody that's really violent, my sister
says. Light flashes on. I panic. The filling station
attendant calms me down but wants to bleed
my brakes. In love's service only the wounded
can serve, a sign says near the Adults Only
Siesta Motel right by Wayne's Half-Price Bedding
with the live goat outside responsible for the yardwork.
Something goes haywire with my right ovary.
The doctor I'm trying this week gives me a prescription
for ultrasound, although I said, Don't bother.
There's a language problem involved. Oh,
that's all right, I said, when he said
after he got the car going, I'll follow you
home. Oh, that's all right, I said,
when as he was leaving he put $5 down
on the table where we eat. You got 10
I said to the woman in group, he gave you 10
for less than 15 minutes and I didn't even get
minimum wage. The paper quotes a prostitute
described only as overweight. I dwell on this.
So, how's the compulsive eating going,
my therapist says to me in one of my best shapeless
unironed outfits after I lose definitely over 12 pounds.

I'm worth it, Cybill Shepherd says in a commercial.
I believe her but I don't believe Elizabeth
Arden who would like me to see a visible
difference. I already tried out-of-character red
bottled color, fuchsia nail paint, green eyeliner.
I scream at sudden sound, movement. I'm tired,
I complain, I want to stop. I think,
my therapist says, as long as you feel
vulnerable, defenseless, you will
scream. Sometimes he can't help himself
being both white and male the way he is but
sometimes I can't find a way in my heart to sympathize
all that much. I'd change the subject but my mind's gone
blank. More than a language barrier holds me still.
I don't say, but I really can't wait for the next life
when I am no longer a woman alone in America,
when I am a great panda in a China with no worry
about a scarcity of young bamboo or nesting
blue eggs on an island somewhere tropical
well out of volcanic range. If I had contracted TB,
instead of only pleurisy, I could be in a sanitarium
somewhere now surrounded by nuns dying with honor
having breakfast in bed and looking more like Audrey
Hepburn every week. Instead, I get nowhere with art
openings or active party liberals. What do you expect,
my sister says, when you don't talk and you don't

make eye contact with anything male over 15. But
I'm willing in this present state to sacrifice almost
anything except probably cigarettes for a good night
with someone else serving guard duty against the dark.
I'm willing to stop using the ironing board as a buffet,
maybe even willing to consider shaving and I
don't care what he doesn't understand. This sounds about
as rational, Karen says, as when you wanted to marry
the therapist. Which I didn't. I just wanted to live
with him and his secretary in his office. For longer
than I would like to remember, it was the only safe place.
Although I never got as far as planning quite what
we would all do with our children. For just $400
I don't have I could invest in a summer social
membership at the club down the street. Cocktails
and the Eddie Clark trio sound like a possible
dentist to me, well over 50 or maybe not
all that particularly well but longing for somebody
else to pick up the dry cleaning. I know
you don't really want one, Karen says.
What would you do with one. But she doesn't have
my nights or my bills. My therapist
has no hope. It would take a special man,
is all he will let himself say. A woman on the beach
today was dying alone of something terrible. Don't
stare, Karen said, but there was almost

nothing left of her and nothing I could do
for her now but remember. My sister
gives me a short skirt. I put it on. There, she says.
Now, don't you feel free.

Perversion

First, I begged him to stop. Then,
for water. For a time I thought that night
I would die sooner of thirst than beneath
his hands. So much later I would rather
not say how much later, I pervert
a careful and simple gesture. A man
places water without comment within my easy
reach. I can not bear even to look at it.
I know I could never in front of him open
my mouth, hold in my mouth water, let a man see
me swallow, let a man see. What is he
trying to do to me, I think. Why is he trying
to torture me, to make my parched heart
bleed.

Some Lucky Girls

We were so lucky to get them. Nobody else
appreciates them. Least of all the professionals who
see this as symptom, wait for anger. But almost
everybody in group agrees. And if some weeks later
some of us stumble around saying I wish he'd killed
me, well, that's just a phase most of us live through
and nobody's paying any attention anyway except
the professionals who offer really good pastel
drugs for both day and night. Of course Louise
I guess basically she always just wanted
to see hers neon flat dead but bleed bad first but
I don't think she ever was really objective of course
there was the matter of that vaginal tear and
he did make her take that supervised bath afterward
but he was so supportive, so sympathetic when
she was getting all upset in the beginning as he
watched her strip standing in her bedroom doorway
he tried to help her through. Rape is never easy, he
said. Caroline and I were crazy about our guys
from the moment they left. My rapist was so nice,
Caroline says. He wanted so very much to please
me. What do you like, he said. I mean, he held a
knife to my throat but he was so gentle. And, my
rapist, he was wonderful. Well, look at me. No
visible scars. He let me live. He let me keep on
my dress.

Man, Woman

He didn't touch you, Paul says. He did not
touch you, Don says.

He fucked you, Barbara says. He really fucked
you, Barbara says. He fucked you. Bad.

Entertaining Ray

Inventing Ray, I fail over and over.
Nothing sounds right. Or true. Except
hunger. Terrible hunger. Even in
the womb I see him, mute mouth moving,
wanting. In the middle of his time
inside me, he held himself perfectly
still and did not look down, but rather
stared straight ahead at blank dimly
lit wall. His face remaining, the way
I see his face always, a face without
expression. Providing no clue to what
he dreams at such times. Do you bowl,
he said. I said, No. I said, No.
I see him now alone at night in the alley.
The forced fall of pins. Line after
line invariably neat and polite as nuns
wearing convent posture. The involuntary
sound they make going down. Ray is
wearing what he always wears. Ray's
clothes do what no one else wants to do.
Hold him. Hold him close and keep
on holding. His narrow body loosens
only in moving away. I leave him there
leaving. As he turns, something haunts
in the way his shoulders shift, sloping
toward an exit.

Hard Evidence

I have been thinking about those shoes. I have
been thinking a lot about those shoes.
I have been thinking about what those shoes mean.
This is what I know. Heavy. Hard. Black. Polished
as much as a shoe polished to start the day
might be with a measure of care at the end of the day.
No one wants to talk with me about those shoes.
Well, Honey, my cousin says, this is sounding
a little obsessed. I really do think you should tell
Craig about this, Bonnie says. She's been
on a first-name basis with my therapist since
we found him together in the Yellow Pages.
I've tried that. He doesn't like talking
about those shoes. I can tell. He just doesn't
understand. I say, Shoes: His whole face just shuts
right down. He doesn't understand those shoes are all
I have. Karen understands. We read the same books.
We both know very very complicated cases solved
in sometimes only 180 pages with nothing but shoes.
Are you in the Navy, I said. Oh, he said,
you mean the shoes. I was just trying
to make conversation. I hadn't noticed anything
about those shoes until Ray said, Oh.
You mean the shoes. That's when I noticed
the shoes. When a sailor dies somewhere
or gets arrested and they put his picture in the paper

I still don't breathe right until I look.
But Karen and I have talked about this.
The question is: Why was he wearing those shoes.
Why wasn't he wearing sneakers like everybody else.
If he had changed out of uniform why was he still
wearing those shoes. But a lot of men
wear shoes like that. Just like that. To work in.
Garbagemen. Garbagemen wear shoes like that.
I have seen garbagemen in my own neighborhood working
in shoes like that. The policewoman says
Ray was just passing through. But you don't
pass along through in shoes like that. I know that.
Karen knows that. We just don't understand why
a trained American policewoman doesn't know that. Why
do you stop at a convenience store late at night wearing
shoes like that. You're on your way home off a swing
shift running a vacuum cleaner or pushing
something that polishes linoleum. I don't think
Ray's in the Navy anymore. I think Ray's
right down the street. Ray was on his way
home wearing those shoes. You mean the shoes, he said,
like he'd said it before. I do this
all the time, he said. I think he does
it on his way home. What have you been thinking
about this week, my therapist says. Well. Those shoes.
Sometimes, I think about those shoes.

I look at him. He is looking
down through his interwoven fingers. He is looking
at his shoes. We both look at his shoes. They're nice
shoes.

Outrageous Behavior

Georgia eggs remain trending unchanged
on mediums; the undertone was steady
at best. Cleveland's donor egg clinic
can not consider a married woman without
her husband's permission. Little done-up
Tammy Faye's reduced to shopping in a
discount outlet store. My therapist is
away again on vacation without me in blue
hill country. A Southside woman last night
fired directly into the abdomen of a still
unidentified man who entered in the usual
way through a window with a knife wanting
to gag, blindfold her using rags. It was
a large caliber gun. He died at 10:30
this morning. Police report no charges
will be filed. Diana appeared in public
in a skintight suit. The color was purple.
The fabric was not disclosed locally. The
first tropical depression of the season
seems in no hurry to move. The heart
of the descending heat pool grows, but lacks
hunger, momentum of its own.

Procedural Similarity

Geographically between Death Row in two states,
baking soda contains the way the day begins:
Frosted Pop Tarts with real fruit filling
ravaged in a toaster oven fire. My legs behave
badly throughout the diaphragm fitting. Other
muscles mislead the physician's assistant into
believing he has a childless woman on his
examining table. This spur of the moment idea's
obviously of the same quality as my teenager's
breakfast. I could have spent this money
on something I can use: Hours on the phone
at daytime rates to Beloit, salon color applied,
another therapy session at the new reduced fee
now the insurance has run out, heightening
performance anxiety while still straining my
balance, making impossible further professional
treatment of the dog's skin condition that defies
both aloe and antibiotics. We have yet to try
wheat germ oil as advised by the health food
store. Preoccupied with my work at slow breathing,
the nurse and I do not, for a while, recognize
wrong reasoning lies behind these so many stabs
at sizing. While she explains what nerves
can do, I forget to inhale. Shallow gasps flash
me rapidly five months back. Then, there was no
woman to hold my hand.

Certain Days, Certain Nights

Sometimes. Still. I want to open my mouth.
Scream.

Unpurchased Batteries

Mid-hurricane season, still lacking on hand
more than half the items my family drug
store advises, along with keeping calm,
as necessary, color emerges with such vengeance
I wonder what it wants. I also wonder why
I need a plastic drop cloth. Is that new, I ask,
stopped and pointing at the small square sofa
I have inhabited for months on a regular basis,
taken by surprise by these sudden flecks
of brightness in this nubby fabric textured
out of someone's vision, perhaps, of a hot
breakfast cereal collage. Finding color
where I expected only the familiar weekly comfort
of whole grain, I realize how I am losing track
of my plots. Even the long night I worked so
hard, busy getting guns to the IRA, is unclear.
Instead, I hold memories of blocks of color,
unnaturally dense: a childhood beach-house wall
but in a yellow previously unknown, an impossibly
pink slab of something, an unavoidable bed
covered to the floor in cranberry or wine or
blood. But there are now at least stories to lose.
The endless round over of nothing but doors,
windows. I travel this weave, remembering.
Between the time of the nightmares and the time
I stopped, for a while, all dreaming, there
was a time of nights without color. Strange

images holding themselves still in black and white.
None of which I remember. Only their eerie lack
of movement. I tried not to. I don't want
to hurt you, he said, but if you move again.
Very cooperative by then, I tried harder, braced
myself somehow still on nothing but worn
carpet. Small raw places were noticed
the next day, puzzling the attending physician and
I was without explanation. The woman there, a new
mother with healthy American hair, who works, of her
own free will and a long ago date gone bad, everyday
with this kind of situation, recognized the marks.
This can be, she said while we were alone together
lunching on food brought in, thin hospital
cafeteria hamburgers and milk, a time of personal
growth. Something which, I explained, in my family
has never particularly been a female goal, meaning
only the kind of expansion caused by too many
quarts consumed in one sitting of homemade maple
walnut ice cream. Rug burn, she said. Rug burn,
he repeated and he wrote it down. Very late
and uncertain, fearing I suppose to face absence,
in the only way I know I squint hard for my aura
until I find along my leg one wide pulsing band,
transparent with a color hard to wear even,
in most cases, as an accessory, that dazzling
lemon-green of very young leaves.

After A Time Consuming Dental Procedure

He pats me, as I am leaving:
Now remember, he says.
If you can lie still through this,
you can lie still through anything.

And I Put Away

                      And I put away
all scent, used only white soap.
And I brought into my house white
flowering plants I then let die so I
did not have to look at them. Each day
look at white flowers and be reminded
I did not feel the way those flowers
looked, I could not remember feeling
the way those flowers looked.

Wild Ribbons

This region gives the national wire cheap filler. Even
our insects are of interest on slow days. A topless
car wash. A topless doughnut shop. Segregated
high-school proms. We like different music, contented
students say. The serial diaper thief still at large.
A fetish, my son is sure, but I am not so certain.
There is a problem with the roof. Whether this is
related to climate, I have no idea but most things here
are. Destruction by water, salt. Eating silver,
art, delicate fabric seems a priority. My son
is happy today. A girl with legs and serious potential
has given him her number. He has gone almost a week
without spilling butterscotch in large quantities
at the fast-food stand. On the beach he reads lines
to me from the magazine that came in the mail. Happily
explaining everything. This is all surrealism. This
is good. This is bad. The introduction to a collection
of seafood recipes moves my sister to tears. I lose
their drift. The twice-convicted diaper thief released
this time for lack of evidence still on my mind.
And another story. One from home. White tulips
wrapped in pink tissue placed at the warm spring scene.
Children gone wild in perfectly pleasant weather. A
young woman, near a pond, near fallen sycamores, nearly
all her blood gone. She had been running in the park
at that hour. That hour is not specified. There is

no need. That hour is a bad hour. To be in the park.
To be at home. To be. There is no good hour. But
this is a pleasant afternoon and that kind of thinking
doesn't really sound very American. I foresee instead
a march down streets with the usual noise, signs.
Take Back the Night. As though time is the matter.
And place. Dark time. Dark streets. Whose interests
do such beliefs serve. But perhaps it is better
we march, better we continue to fail this quiz. Where
does it usually happen. a) home b) street. When
does it usually happen. a) day b) night. Delusion
is necessary for mental health, claims the article
my mother sends. I have lived this way all my life,
my still married mother writes in the margin with
exclamation points. The wife of our new vice president
has chosen her project. Preparedness for disaster.
There are many tracks open women today in America.
In Israel a witness testifies: It was then we found
women and children burn that easily. Somewhere
I think I read this still breathing and therefore
in all good taste still nameless young woman
was on a fast track. I hope so. I truly do hope so.
Very fast. Very bright. I can see her. Flying
home. Wild bare arms breaking bright ribbons free.

Multiple Choice

Ray says he is

a) vacationing from Virginia.

b) from Louisiana.

c) newly transferred by the Navy from California.

The policewoman says
most likely
Ray is

d) none of the above.

The policewoman says
most likely
Ray is

not Ray.

First Recital

    I go to my room. I take off
the dress. I hang up the dress at the end
of the closet. I don't know what I do
with the bra. I think I take it off. I'm
pretty sure I took it off. I don't know
when I collect the other things from the living
room floor. I know the shoes stayed
where they were for a while because I remember
one day they surprised me. I saw them
and I thought what are my shoes doing out
here and then I remembered and I put them
away. As though preparing for weather,
although this is Florida where they haven't
had any in years but natives say it's time
again for a tropical storm to ransack this coast
with voices betraying memories oblivious to lack
of running water and light, I put on white cotton
underpants, hand-me-down jeans of my son, one
of his oxford cloth shirts diluted navy and white
vertical stripes, his navy cotton crew-neck
sweater that swallows me, my own white cotton
socks and canvas sneakers. When my son says
he always knows where to look for his clothes,
I tell him I don't know how they get in here.
Laundry just goes astray on you sometimes. But
he is young and doesn't understand that yet. I

go with the dog into my son's room where he is
not sleeping because he is sleeping in his cousin's
room in my sister's house. I get on the floor
with the phone book. Somehow it opens to a page
that lists Rape Crisis Hotline in bold type.
I dial. The woman who answers tells me she isn't
Rape Crisis anymore. She's another hotline.
She gives me another number. I dial. A recording
tells me Rape Crisis Hotline has a new number. I
dial. The new number has been disconnected.
I call the police. I say I don't want to report
anything or anything like that but I was just
wondering if you might happen to have a number
for something like a rape hotline. The man gets
off the phone. There is talk in the background.
He gets back on the line. He gives me a number.
It is the number in the phone book. I look
at the clock. Everywhere in America it is still
the middle of the night. I dial Wisconsin
where my best friend since sixth grade in suburban
Connecticut and Miss Donna's ballet class lives now
a time zone away. Julie says, Hello. I say, Rape.
Julie says, What. I say, Rape. Julie says, What.
I spell it. Oh, Julie says, rape. No one says
anything. For the real life sound of her, I
ask about the weather. We talk then of winter

in Beloit and how she is wearing her hair now.
Still a blunt cut but a little shorter in the back.
Julie won't let me go until I promise to leave
the house, go to my sister's. While promising
I know I am able to go nowhere and it is nowhere
near dawn.

Baskets.

Even I like this. Yes. With
my hands. My hands my sisters eye
what is held expecting
damage.
This form so unlike
speech in this no longer comfortable
language
feels natural as braiding
young family hair.
Form belonging only
to ourselves. Requiring no explanation.
Because it happened here I begin with
what is here. Palm. And because
of what happened to my own palm.
Palm and branches of available roses.
Painted paper. Paper painted
by my sister with the small floral pattern
of the discarded dress. Purple, white, green,
blue. The last dress she helped me find.
The one even I felt feminine inside. I
hardly ever wear one any more. Barbara
notices. Misunderstands
the repetition of a few safe clothes. Always
loose. Never ironed. Announces
she is going to do what I do. Wear
just anything she wants. I am reminded:

Want has had little
to do with my recent life. Nothing
to do with my wardrobe. I wear
what I can. Clothes as symptom not
statement. I do not complete
the oval. Leave the slope of shape
open. Or, unfinished.
But this is not just
another broken object in the house.
Remembrance does not basket up neatly.
I assumed weaving might guide me somewhere
beyond language.
I believed I believed if I made this basket if
I held the rape in my hands.
I suppose I hoped to feel
something. Actual
tears. Not expecting
just the usual
bloodshed. Cut up hands.
Unwise choice of material.
I study my palms
the broken lifeline the line that split
marked proof death of the raped woman is
no fantasy. The body knows more than the world.
This fading line remains.
Reminds me:

There is an unburied woman in this house.

A body is denying a woman a marked grave.

The lifeline sometimes splits, it says

in Elementary Palmistry, when there is

a move to another country.

I love you, Donald says. I love you,

Barbara says. I say

nothing. Want only

to get away.

I don't know the woman

they talk about and they never met

the woman I can almost on a good day remember

being.

I am reminded:

A woman deserves a grave. The body needs

to cry. The palm conceals nothing.

Bread, Water

Unfamiliar with a household still stocking white
bread, still, for whatever reason, it is white bread
I see in her hands. "Tuesday, I ate two slices.
In my room, I keep water." Useless in these
circumstances to survey progress with those other
complicated rituals: sleeping, washing, dressing. We
exchange family news. A woman inmate is to die
here on my sister's birthday. Trouble with the shower
was only an accumulation of sand, not the collapsed
pipes my brother-in-law suspected. The antique
jam jars she found for her mother remain misplaced.
We do not speculate on the current appetite of the
man who scaled a wall wanting he said to make her
happy.

Aberrational Manners

Please.

The lie: I just want to touch it.

Please.

The lie, followed by endearment: Baby, baby.

Please.

The endearment, followed by lie: Baby, we're both saying please.

Please.

The lie, followed by, followed by, followed by:

Kiss me. Kiss me. I don't want to hurt you. Kiss me.

I'm just touching it. Kiss me. Why

won't you kiss me. Kiss me. Please.

Please.

Spotting Ray

The day I spot Ray lounging in the doorway of Harry's
boarded-up pawn shop, my therapist leaves town for
a death in the family. I drive by Harry's every day
on the way to work through that sorry stretch of
downtown. Around Harry's lately I nurse swallowing
a washed-out and bitter orange pill, whose bottle says
as needed for anxiety. It's a taste I've acquired.
Harry's been up for sale for a while now, but I've
never seen Ray by there before. Ray was looking
pretty good in battle fatigues. The beard all still
there he said he planned to shave. Why, I said, it's
a good beard. Keep it. Wondering could I ever
positively identify him without it. I look back, long
as I dare, knowing I need to keep my eyes' custody on
the road. But I want to roll my window down and wave,
Hey. I want eye contact when I say, Who have you
buried, Ray. Instead, I remember skipping the cemetery
to go directly from Mass to my grandmother's house,
charged by my sister with care of her cobalt enameled
casserole, along with warming her sweet marinated
chicken hors d'oeuvres, famous at family funeral
parties. Trouble lighting the gas oven loses me
some eyebrow, singes edges of my hair. I lose my
sister's directions in the mirror above the bathroom
sink, convincing myself everyone will be too distraught
and who in the family has enough sight left anyway

to notice. If caught, I'll say I got carried away
with plucking. But even skirting the get-together's edge
I can't miss what my sister has to say about her
scorched enamel. Daddy's first cousin, Helen, whose hair
remembers waving passion bright, doesn't let me slip
past. How are you, Honey, she says. Fine, thank you,
Helen, I say, and you. Helen takes me by the shoulders,
looks me in the eye. No, Honey, she says. Your grandfather
you loved, who loved you, is dead. Honey, you are not
fine. In the doorway of the room where he left his body
in his own bed, in his own sleep, we lean into one
another, looking out into the kitchen. When it was
linoleumed red, he stood singing there. For me.

The Color Of The Rug

What color is the rug.
Terrible, I said.
I know, he said, I know.
But what color.
Horrible, I said.

Real Life

But in real life, I begin. But Doug
interrupts: What happened that night was
real life. I don't know what he is
talking about. Real life is my sister
studying the bankruptcy notices each week
in the paper and continuing to have
difficulty with her soft consonants.
My psychic finding in the cards arrows
of love, waters of life. My son saying
I am the most dimwitted person he knows
and bringing home from a concert a pair
of bottled blondes from Mississippi,
escapees from a senior trip, who refuse
to respond to my questions—Where
is the rest of the class. Where are
your chaperones. Rinsing dishes
in the bathroom sink after the kitchen
faucet explodes without warning and, tired
of Electra shedding on the blue Chinese
plates, working to clear in the cabinet
space some builder allotted without
me in mind a shelf she can call her own.
Real life is Diana writing from Head
of the Tide, Maine, she is having a good
time fixing broken furniture and lamps.
Mary Kay eating potato chips with raisins

still so mad with the father of her children
for coming down with pneumonia after that
camping trip when she was the one who
deserved it. Bonnie, after reconciling
with a man denied tenure, making humming
sounds swallowing lettuce spread with jam.
In real life, a girlchild swings from the
flowering tree branching out over my terrace.
You know the secret of trees, she calls down
to her friend. You want one, you
find one. In real life, my chest tightens
and I forgive all the white blossoms
her careless legs have sent to the ground.
Not this girl. Never this girl. Not
in real life.

Color Study

The same day my therapist surprises me in blue
suspenders buttoned to khaki trousers, I
am thinking about blue things. I am thinking
of painting everything shades of tropical water.
Katie writes she is also thinking. She is
planning menus, although her schedule allows
no time for cooking. Meanwhile, Nancy arrives,
her hair as soft in my hands as I remember,
to feed me New England winter meals. She bakes
me foods the color of her hair—carrots
and acorn squash halved, filled with real
butter and touched with nutmeg—along with
the white food I favor—potatoes, onions,
chicken. She leaves but leaves me these
foods to come back to, only needing to be warmed
to give me mouthfuls of home. But the food
runs out. I turn back to sandwiches and all
my little plastic bottles. Prescribed aqua.
Peach. Blue. My sister drops by her chatterbox
self, done-up starched in that thick white
blouse I like so much. The one she complains
about: the cleaners never get the pleats quite
right and that statistics class is ruining
her life. I feed my pretty sister sliced chicken
with mayonnaise on good French bread and Florida
oranges.

Common Expression

The man above me is saying something. He is
saying something over and over the same
thing. What. What are you saying, I am
saying but he is still saying what
he was saying using the sound of it to take him
where he wants to go and someplace inside me
closes and I feel nothing but know only this
cheap chosen comfort has taken a sudden twist
straight toward the worst. And all this is now
is waiting for it please to stop. Escape turned
reenactment out of nothing but one
word of language. But I don't know
that yet. I don't know that
until morning when I remember when
I heard that word before come
over and over out of a man's mouth
like that just like that.
In the afternoon sounds I can not place
keep coming out of me.
I remember not knowing
what would happen
when he stopped. Life
or death was all I thought was
at stake. Who could have imagined
this.

Here, Among Old Roses

Traditionally depicted, the Roman god of silence
holds a white rose. There is no white rose
in my hand. Let us pray. "We are
the stories we tell." I believe that. Believe that.
What then happens to us when the stories we are
remain unspoken. I am the story I tell and I can tell you
to need story and find only absence or worse lies
what happens to self, to vision, to world is
unimaginable. As for what happens to the heart,
what happened to my heart, you ask my sister, who
every day holds me, holds me and says, good girl,
you're a good girl, you are such a good girl, knowing
I can not believe her, not knowing
if I will ever believe her, if the sister she holds
will always only be the shell, all soul scooped out of a woman
she alone remembers and I do not remember.
But I don't have to tell you that. I am not this story
alone. This story is our story. Let us pray.
Rinse your hands with rose water. With your hands in my hands,
here, among pagan trees, among old roses—weeping,
climbing, wild—together, here, we will pray language.
Let us begin. Let us pray in required sunlight.
We are not here to consider the appeal of mute ruins,
the hollowness of reason, the veneer of American order.
And, we already understand the many meanings of whiteness.
This garden is not about charm nor the mathematics
of living form. This is about survival, something
old roses understand. Telling the story, we are.

Final Words

I know you may not believe me, he said. But
I'll be out there. I'll be out there. I'll be
waiting for you.

What Backlash

I

For a Year of the Woman issue, a magazine prints
some full color portraits of some American women.
Hillary Clinton is on the floor.
Tipper Gore is looking in a mirror.
Hillary Clinton is on the floor.
Tipper Gore is looking in a mirror.
Hillary Clinton is on the floor.
Tipper Gore is looking in a mirror.
Yeah, get right down there on the floor, Bill.
Oh, Al, let's get one of you looking in that mirror.

II

But, why did they do it, my mother says. Why
did they do it.
I have forgotten.
This is America.
Let us now discuss the responsibility
of the victim.
But, why did she keep working for him.
But, why did she go up to his hotel room.
But, why did she drive that boy home
from a bar in the middle of the night.
But, why did she go into his house.

But, why did they pick that cotton.
Why don't we all just relax,
pass around the current cool wine and sing
something patriotic.

The Plague

My son finds *The Plague* wilder than anything
by Kafka stuck with metaphors always his own
personal life. I of course understand
none of this nor why facing the very real
prospect of a summerful of chemistry with no
scrap of homework started he is still talking
diagonal in the dark of all things at 9:33 with
Jen who has yet to commit to the prom. She can't
find the dress after how many times have I
screamed Jacobson's Junior Department loud
enough to carry across the wires of the best
telephone system in the world even dismantled
now the way it is or it's not Morning
in America. The only source of the news I want
reports Assassins Stalk the Young Royals narrowly
missing Charles with that recent avalanche
denying Diana a stab at a man who knows how
to fast dance which proves my mother's point
although she wants my opinion but Great Aunt Sally
agrees the book is written in the womb. Why
else is the prince not buried. While I am
thinking what mother do you know would carry this
book to term why live birth would all but cease,
I have on good authority Mary is on her way
to dying of burnt pan syndrome outside
of Boston confirming I can be a complete woman

with limited kitchen involvement. Trauma
in the general region induces a perfect case
of pleurisy diagnosed in scuffed up Nikes
by Doctor Dale partial to coed health
club Jacuzzis so he can in his own words talk
to girls for $38 and the chance to listen
to my heart is it too much to expect grown-up
shoes a familiar condition in my mother's
family with signs torn between hysterical
pregnancy and American female depression mass
market paperbacks tell me is epidemic. No one
can imagine why or what for that matter
Jesse might possibly want but then who alive
remembers the early '60s when with 40% of our
women seriously believed frigid researchers
dosed the chosen with LSD yielding the miracle
of vaginal orgasms on demand but beauty
treatments can't hurt my sister announces
as she signs us up for Monday morning
pedicures with Lily who doesn't believe in
moisturizing dry skin it's senseless to relieve
the dominant symptom pain aggravated by simple
breathing I found a daily trial to want
in the early aftermath over a year ago now
and certainly don't you think my therapist must
have been joking when he said last week I'm

Republican. Although I can't say I've ever been
entirely free of concern since the day
shock's veil lifted sufficiently for me
to recognize I was receiving treatment I called
comfort in a house painted blue. Even granting
the scope of pastel acceptability in this
place some circumstances test faith. But
if my father can believe a novena with or
in these contemporary times without candle
prayed Tuesday afternoons to my sister's
namesaint solves his life I can surely believe
it came blue and the absence of animal hair
on his jackets represents a temporary
affliction. It could happen to anyone. It
could happen to Molly who writes a Letter
to the Editor ending I walk in good lighting
and never alone. I will not be a victim.

Page 134

The paperback fires itself out of my hands. I jump
around back and forth like something caged
making mostly noise without words except:
No. No. No. This is over 2,000 days later. This
is the kind of scene you never want witnessed.
This is the first time I see Ray's last name in print.
I never find him in my phone book. Although each year
when the new one comes, some late night finds me hunched,
searching. The name is common, Cajun, thinks
the New Orleans homicide detective studying her list
of serial killer suspects. Four days later, I get out
my French dictionary. Repeating his name, I said,
how do you spell that and I remember being reminded
of French blue. The word is not there. Nothing, nothing
like the word is there. Alone in my house, I am screaming.
It doesn't mean anything. It doesn't mean anything.

Market Research

My thermal carafe coffeemaker comes
with a 16 page instructional manual and a survey.
Do you or anyone in your household
own or plan to purchase:
a cordless handheld vacuum, a smoke alarm, a rechargeable light.
To help us understand our customers' lifestyles
please indicate the interests and activities
in which you or your partner enjoy participating
on a regular basis:
vegetable gardening, fashion clothing, casino gambling, group therapy.
Please check all that apply to your household:
support health charities, purchase items through the mail, train dogs.
My answers will be used anonymously in market research.
My answers will allow me to receive mailings and special offers
that relate directly to my specific interests.
The survey doesn't ask:
Do you have difficulty retaining domestic help.
Do you believe the following are your fault:
your son's math grades, the dog's skin condition, failure of the ERA.
Do you open your windows.
When someone knocks, do you open your door.
The survey doesn't ask:
Do you ever anywhere anytime believe yourself safe.
The survey doesn't ask:
Are you a woman in America.

All Of This Happens In A Warm Coastal Climate.

Angela rubs her walls, ceilings seclusion blue.

Wears another woman's dresses, dreams real stories

from another woman's life. Productions of stage

classics in which she waits in the wings.

Without lines.

Katie folds paper, remains indoors.

Unpacked boxes from the move south

deny her a bedroom for several years. She concentrates

on ethical vegetarianism and her new art form. Paper

without words.

I keep rape scraps in a small white paper bag.

Pieces of carpet cut out with scissors, labeled

with permanent marker. This happened here. This happened.

Events coded not in letters, but in scrawled designs

because there are

no names

for that or for most of what shades a woman's life.

Dialogue attempts falter. One necessary soul remains always

absent. And when the examined wound is unwashable.

What then. When no sacrament exists.

When homemade ritual seems only that.

Not close enough is as close as we ever get to whatever truth is.

Let alone might set free.

Even our analyst loses patience, heart. Decides

to relocate far away from water, humidity, us.

Gives up translation of incoherent traumatized women

without cars.

Women who breathe too fast, can not meet his eyes, gesture wildly, regularly endangering his lamps, always almost breaking something irreplaceable.

Takes up the more pure, more accessible language of mathematics.

Genuine art. And respectable.

And we, with this habit we now have of being left

still alive,

confide to one another one another's secrets, never

our own.

Blade. Drug. Cliff. Oven. Waves. Rope. The recurring

lost audition.

Without notes.

None of us can write.

We just read.

Public records, tabloids. Imagine perfect endings. Everybody gets

a speaking part.

Automatic Icemaker

"He saw something he liked." That's good
enough to get you out of kindergarten
in the state of Florida, where to get a chance
with the written word a certified classroom
teacher needs to hear you get five recognizable
words into a complete sentence. The sentence
need not be true. "He saw something he liked."
A brother talks on late night television
about the man who murdered his sister.
When he delivered her refrigerator, "he saw
something he liked." What is wrong
with that sentence. If you don't feel
up to that one, let me read out loud to you
a sentence Bonnie read out loud to me.
She found this sentence in a helpful book.
"If you are reading this, you did everything
right." What is wrong with that sentence.
If you don't feel up to that one, just tell me
this: Do you ever think Sarah might just maybe
give us that cake recipe.

Dear Susan,

"I am not the person who set off, singing,
on that sunny Fourth of July in the French countryside.
I left her
in a muddy creekbed at the bottom of a ravine.
I had to."

Dear Susan,
I, also, left her.
I left her on the floor in my own house.
Cooperative girls, they stay where we leave them.
She sits there still on debris colored carpet in her pretty dress.
Her face, turned toward the window, sees nothing.
We abandon ourselves. Name this survival.
And the planet litters with women abandoned women.

And so, yes, we, mostly, survive. But Susan,
surviving seems no "accomplishment" to me, no "honor."
Only really bad luck.
Just some clever contemporary alternative spelling of exile.
Our forged afterwards too costly. Worthless. Worthless.

In the obituary of actress Eugenie Leontovich,
I read the explanation of her daily costuming in black:
She quoted Chekov, "I am in mourning for my life."
Given time, the tragic turns tiresome. Or worse,
an exile's affectation.

That She May

1690
Guilt being nothing else but trouble arising in our minds,
from a consciousness of having done contrary to what we are
verily perswaded was our Duty.
—Tillotson

1992
While prior to the rape they had been no more likely
than anyone else to attempt suicide, almost one in five
made a suicide attempt following the rape.
—Herman

1647
That she may guiltless of it live.
—Cowley

1390
She taketh up in her self the gilt.
—Gower

One in five attempt.
That she may guiltless of it live. One in five attempt.
She taketh up in her self the guilt. One in five attempt.

1992.

The fifth February.

Trouble arises in my mind.

I am in

really bad

trouble.

Are you suicidal, Donald says.

I don't know

the right answer.

I don't know

what being suicidal means.

One in five attempt. That she may guiltless of it
live. One in five attempt. She taketh up in her
self the guilt. One in five attempt.

Does it mean

each night

while walking with the dog

saying

I can't bear this.

I am going to have to die

because

I can't bear

this.

One in five attempt. That she may
guiltless of it live. One in five attempt.
She taketh up in her self the guilt.
One in five attempt.

Does it mean
each night
saying
Nothing, no one can help me.
No one. Nothing.
I am going to have to
die.

One in five attempt.
That she may guiltless of it live.
One in five attempt.
She taketh up in her self the guilt.
One in five attempt.

Does it mean
each night
saying
Is this what happens.
Is this the way we die.
Is this what happens.

After all this, all this
and now, now I am
going to have to die.

Does that mean
being suicidal.
I have no plan.
I don't want to die.
It's just
that I'm going to have to.
So, I say,
No. No.
And feel
guilty.
Maybe
no
isn't really
the right answer.

One in five attempt. That she may
guiltless of it
live.
One in five. One in five. One in five.
She taketh up in her self
the guilt.

How did it happen, Donald says.
Oh, it was my fault, I say. It was all
my fault. It was my fault.
How did it happen, he says.
Oh, I can't tell you that, I say.
I can't tell you that.
I could never
tell you
that.
It was my fault.

You can tell me,
Donald says, you can tell
me.
And so, we begin.

That she may. That she may.

Vocabulary Words

The woman is ovulating. On the floor, she knows this. She
has never seen beneath the microscope the shapes of ferns
cervical secretions assume only at this time. But
she imagines them. Male ferns, you know, are common
as mud. She imagines only uncommon ferns.
Maiden's hair. Venus hair. Heart's tongue.
Cinnamon. Slender cliff. Madeline. Madeline.
Jennifer Anne. Ovulating, the woman dreams
a story. In that first garden, where they slept
they slept among ferns in weather we call
spring and ferns were the meal she prepared
for them the day she first conceived and the first music
in the garden was the sound humming its way out of her
during the conceiving, conjuring crystal spiral
unfurling. On the floor, the woman has forgotten
her story, her possible daughters. She has not forgotten
she is ovulating. The man is stopping
touching her now. The man tells the woman on the floor
she has to do something for him now. But first,
he offers to do something else for her. No. Threatens
to do. There were no offers that night. When the man
knocked the woman to the floor her mouth dried. This
is what desert, death mean now to her. This night, this man
is what terror means now to her. Time will expand
this definition to night and men. She is learning
real meanings of common words, here, this night,

on the floor. On the floor, she will beg this night
for water. Years later, talking alone in a closed room
with a man her mouth will dry. She will not ask a man again
for water. The woman on the floor believes she has a choice
of what to lose. Does what he has been wanting
her to do. She kisses him to keep his mouth
away from her. She will continue to kiss him to keep
sure of his mouth's whereabouts. She knows, reaching
for his mouth, she is losing this. The woman
on the floor is kissing the man who has her
down on the floor. She feels nothing. She
feels nothing so when she sees him coming
out of her and she has felt nothing, known
nothing, she goes a little maybe you'd say crazy.
The woman on the floor is making noise and the woman
is ovulating. On the floor, she knows this.
She begs the man. She will not stop. She will not stop.
She does not beg him to stop. She knows now he will
not stop until he stops. She knows when he stops he will
kill her but maybe he will not kill her maybe
she will still be alive when he stops and she is
ovulating. She begs him to let her put in her
diaphragm. During this time, he has been moving
her, slamming parts of her into what does not
move—wall, furniture, door—pushing her
along the carpet the way you push

hard on a rag wiping a bad kitchen
and each time the man starts to raise himself above the woman
to do what a man does above a woman
the woman has been trying to move underneath him,
all scatter and confusion in the darkness
like some blind little animal
trying to maybe scramble herself maybe somehow away and
trying to avoid him and she does not know if she is
avoiding him because she feels nothing
and the man is pressing down on her so hard
so hard scraping her into place to keep her
still. The man is not confused. The man is not pleased.
The man is not pleased with the woman's behavior. He
lets her know that. He lets her know that. He lets her
know her behavior will have to improve. The man tells
the woman he does not want to hurt her. He
tells her what he does not want to have to do to her,
what he does not want to have to make her do. He
reminds the woman of what he was willing to do
for her, is still willing to do. He would do that, he says,
for her. The woman on the floor can not improve
her behavior but she promises. She promises and the man
decides to allow her the diaphragm. He stands. He looks
down at her. He looks down at her. He tells her she can
get up. He asks if she wants him to help her get up.
She says no. She says she can get up. These words

do not really come out of her mouth. What
comes out of her is only a slur of sound
but the man understands this language. She
gets up. She is standing. She falls to the floor.
A little heap. He offers to help her up. She says
no. She says she can get up by herself. She
tries. She tries to get up. She is almost now
what you could almost call almost standing. She falls again.
The man says nothing. He picks her up. He holds her
standing against him. Holding her, holding
her arms, he half-carries her into the bathroom her hand
gestures him toward. She scans surfaces, opens cabinets.
She can not find the diaphragm. She finds the diaphragm. He
asks if he can help. She says no. He says he wants
to help. She says no. He contents himself with holding
her dress up around her waist. She gets
the diaphragm in. It is over now. She knows this.
He must know now what he has been doing. It is over now.
She knows this. He will leave. The man pushes her back
into the living room. The man tells her she has to get back
down on the floor now. The woman can not believe
this is happening. She believes this is happening.
She believes he still must not know what he is doing.
At the same time she believes he does not know
what he is doing she believes he knows
what he is doing and she believes he will kill her. There

is a word for this simultaneous belief in incongruous
notions. He makes her get down on the floor.
He will keep her, there, on the floor
two more hours. When he leaves he leaves her
alive. When he leaves he leaves her a five-dollar bill.
When he leaves he leaves her in such good condition
when people say did he hurt you, she can honestly say,
No. He did not hurt me.

I never again consult my fern lover's companion.
The meaning of ovulation has been changed for me.

This Will Happen.

Why did rape capture you. Why did it capture
your life.

When your hand was cut, why did your hand
bleed.

Island Of The Raped Women

There are no paved roads here and all of the goats
are well-behaved. Mornings, beneath thatched shelters,
we paint wide-brimmed straw hats. We paint them
inside and outside. We paint very very fast. Five
hats a morning. We paint very very slow. One hat
a week. All of our hats are beautiful and we all look
beautiful in our hats. Afternoons, we take turns:
mapping baby crabs moving in and out of sand, napping,
baking. We make orange and almond cake. This requires
essence and rind. Whipped cream. Imagination.
We make soft orange cream. This requires juice
of five oranges and juice of one lemon. (Sometimes
we substitute lime for the lemon. That is also good.)
An enamel lined pan. Four egg yolks and four ounces
of sugar. This requires careful straining, constant
stirring, gentle whisking. Watching for things not
to boil. Waiting for things to cool. We are good
at this. We pour our soft orange cream into custard
cups. We serve this with sponge cake. Before
dinner, we ruffle pink sand from one another's hair.
This feels wonderful and we pretend to find the results
interesting. We all eat in moderation and there is no
difficulty swallowing. We go to bed early. (Maybe, we
even turn off lights. Maybe, we even sleep naked. Maybe.)
We all sleep through the night. We wake eager from dreams

filled with blue things and designs for hats.
At breakfast, we make a song, chanting our litany
of so much collected blue. We do not talk of going
back to the world. We talk of something else
sweet to try with the oranges: Sponge custard.
Served with thick cream or perhaps with raspberry sauce.
We paint hats. We paint hats.

Books from **Pleasure Boat Studio**

William Slaughter, THE POLITICS OF MY HEART
  Fall 1996 (ISBN 0-9651413-0-6)

Frances Driscoll, THE RAPE POEMS
  Spring 1997 (ISBN 0-9651413-1-4)

Michael Blumenthal, WHEN HISTORY ENTERS THE HOUSE
  Fall 1997 (ISBN 0-9651413-2-2)

from **Pleasure Boat Studio**
an essay written by Ouyang Xiu,
Song dynasty poet, essayist, and scholar,
on the twelfth day of the twelfth month
in the *renwu* year (January 25, 1043)

*I have heard of men of antiquity who fled from the world to distant rivers
and lakes and refused to their dying day to return. They must have found
some source of pleasure there. If one is not anxious for profit, even at the
risk of danger, or is not convicted of a crime and forced to embark; rather,
if one has a favorable breeze and gentle seas and is able to rest
comfortably on a pillow and mat, sailing several hundred miles in a single
day, then is boat travel not enjoyable? Of course, I have no time for such
diversions. But since 'pleasure boat' is the designation of boats used for
such pastimes, I have now adopted it as the name of my studio. Is there
anything wrong with that?*

Translated by Ronald Egan
THE LITERARY WORKS OF OU-YANG HSIU
Cambridge University Press
New York 1984